Jesus

The Teacher

**Matthew 3:13-17, 4:1-17, 5:1-48, 6:1-15,
7:1-23, 11:1-30, 12:1-8, 18:1-20, 19:13-26,
25:31-46; Mark 1:9-11, 2:23-28, 4:21-23,
9:33-37, 10:13-16; Luke 3:21,22, 6:1-49,
9:46-48, 18:15-17**

by

Rebecca Daniel

illustrated by

Nancee McClure

A Christian Education Activity Book

Cover by Nancee McClure
Copyright © Good Apple, Inc., 1984

ISBN No. 0-86653-225-0
Printing No. 9876543

Shining Star Publications
A Division of Good Apple, Inc.
Box 299
Carthage, IL 62321-0299

NOTE: The activities in this book were written using the King James Version of the Bible, so always use this version to solve the puzzles.

INTRODUCTION

Jesus was a wonderful teacher! Everywhere He went, people gathered around Him to hear His wisdom. Jesus was baptized by His cousin, John. "And Jesus, when he was baptized, went up straightway out of the water: and, lo, the heavens were opened unto him, and he saw the Spirit of God descending like a dove, and lighting upon him: And lo a voice from heaven, saying, This is my beloved Son, in whom I am well pleased."

Being assured by the Holy Spirit, Jesus went into the wilderness alone to plan His work for establishing God's kingdom. After forty days and nights, the devil tempted Jesus. The devil said, "If thou be the Son of God, command that those stones be made bread." Jesus answered the devil with these words: "It is written, Man shall not live by bread alone, but by every word that proceedeth out of the mouth of God." Again the devil tempted Jesus: "If thou be the Son of God, cast thyself down." The devil wanted to see if angels would rescue Jesus. "Jesus said unto him, It is written again, Thou shalt not tempt the Lord thy God." Next the devil offered the world and glory to Jesus if Jesus would worship him. "Then saith Jesus unto him, Get thee hence, Satan: for it is written, Thou shalt worship the Lord thy God, and him only shalt thou serve. Then the devil leaveth him, and, behold, angels came and ministered unto him."

One day Jesus climbed a little way up the side of a mountain. He called His disciples around Him. Many other people had followed. Jesus sat down and taught them the rules of belonging to God's kingdom. He said, "Blessed are the poor in spirit: for their's is the kingdom of heaven. Blessed are they that mourn: for they shall be comforted. Blessed are the meek: for they shall inherit the earth. Blessed are they which do hunger and thirst after righteousness: for they shall be filled. Blessed are the merciful: for they shall obtain mercy. Blessed are the pure in heart: for they shall see God. Blessed are the peacemakers: for they shall be called the children of God. Blessed are they which are persecuted for righteousness' sake: for their's is the kingdom of heaven. Blessed are ye, when men shall revile you, and persecute you, and shall say all manner of evil against you falsely, for my sake. Rejoice, and be exceeding glad: for great is your reward in heaven: for so persecuted they the prophets which were before you."

During His travels, Jesus often stopped to pray. One day the disciples asked Jesus to teach them how to pray. Jesus taught them this prayer: "Our Father which art in heaven, Hallowed be thy name. Thy kingdom come. Thy will be done in earth, as it is in heaven. Give us this day our daily bread. And forgive us our debts, as we forgive our debtors. And lead us not into temptation, but deliver us from evil: For thine is the kingdom, and the power, and the glory, for ever. Amen."

Jesus taught people how to have faith. "Ask, and it shall be given you; seek, and ye shall find; knock, and it shall be opened unto you." Jesus said many things about love. He taught a new commandment: "Love your enemies, bless them that curse you, do good to them that hate you." Jesus especially loved children. He called them "the greatest in the kingdom of heaven." He taught that to do good to others is like doing good to Him. "Verily I say unto you, Inasmuch as ye have done it unto one of the least of these my brethren, ye have done it unto me."

FORTY DAYS AND FORTY NIGHTS

Matthew 3:13-17, 4:1-17; Mark 1:9-11; Luke 3:21,22

Use the number code to solve this puzzle.

A=1, B=2, C=3, D=4, E=5, F=6, G=7, H=8, I=9,
J=10, K=11, L=12, M=13, N=14, O=15, P=16,
Q=17, R=18, S=19, T=20, U=21, V=22, W=23,
X=24, Y=25, Z=26

"13,1,14   19,8,1,12,12   14,15,20   12,9,22,5

____   _____   ___   ____

2,25   2,18,5,1,4   1,12,15,14,5."   "20,8,15,21

__   _____   _____   ____

19,8,1,12,20   14,15,20   20,5,13,16,20   20,8,5

_____   ___   _____   ___

12,15,18,4   20,8,25   7,15,4."   "7,5,20

____   ___   ___   ___

20,8,5,5   8,5,14,3,5 ,   19,1,20,1,14."

____   ____   _____

Name_____

Let the Scriptures help you solve this crossword puzzle.

"Then saith Jesus (5 across) him, Get thee hence, Satan: for it is (1 down), Thou (7 down) (1 across) the Lord thy God, and (8 down) only shalt thou (2 down). Then the (3 across) (4 down) him, and, behold, (6 across) came and (9 across) unto him."

Matthew 4:10,11

What word found in the Scriptures can you put in the top row that makes three-letter words of the letters going down?

e	v	a	a	o	i	w	n	n	o
a	e	d	n	o	m	o	n	e	t

Name_____

Shining Star Publication, Copyright © 1984, A division of Good Apple, Inc.

SERMON ON THE MOUNT

Matthew 5:1-12

Add the correct vowel in each blank to spell words and discover the secret message.

"__ nd   s __ __ __ ng   th __
m __ lt __ t __ d __ s,   h __   w __ nt   __ p
__ nt __   __   m __ __ nt __ __ n: __ nd
wh __ n   h __   w __ s   s __ t,   h __ s
d __ sc __ pl __ s   c __ m __   __ nt __
h __ m: __ nd   h __   __ p __ n __ d
h __ s   m __ __ th,   __ nd   t __ __ ght
th __ m . . . ."

Name_____

Shining Star Publication, Copyright © 1984, A division of Good Apple, Inc.

Draw a line to connect the appropriate words. Use your Bible to help you. Then write the letters that fall at each line intersection to discover the secret word.

SECRET WORD: __ __ __

poor in spirit •   • comforted

P   G   O

they that mourn •   • kingdom of heaven

S   T

meek •   • the earth

I   A

hunger & thirst
for righteousness •   • obtain mercy

N   O   M

merciful •   • shall be filled

pure in heart •   F   • called the
                                                   children of God

D   C

peacemakers •   • shall see God

Can you spell 12 words mentioned in the Scriptures using only the letters in the box found below?

H	A	E
W	S	D
N	T	R

_____   _____

_____   _____

_____   _____

_____   _____

Name_____

SIMILITUDES

Matthew 5:17-30; Mark 4:21-23; Luke 6: 20-49

To discover the secret message, follow each line and write the letters in the order they are found.

SECRET MESSAGE: __ ___

__ __ __ __ __ __ __ __ __

__ __ __ __ __ __ __, __ __ __ __ __

__ __ __ __ __ __ .

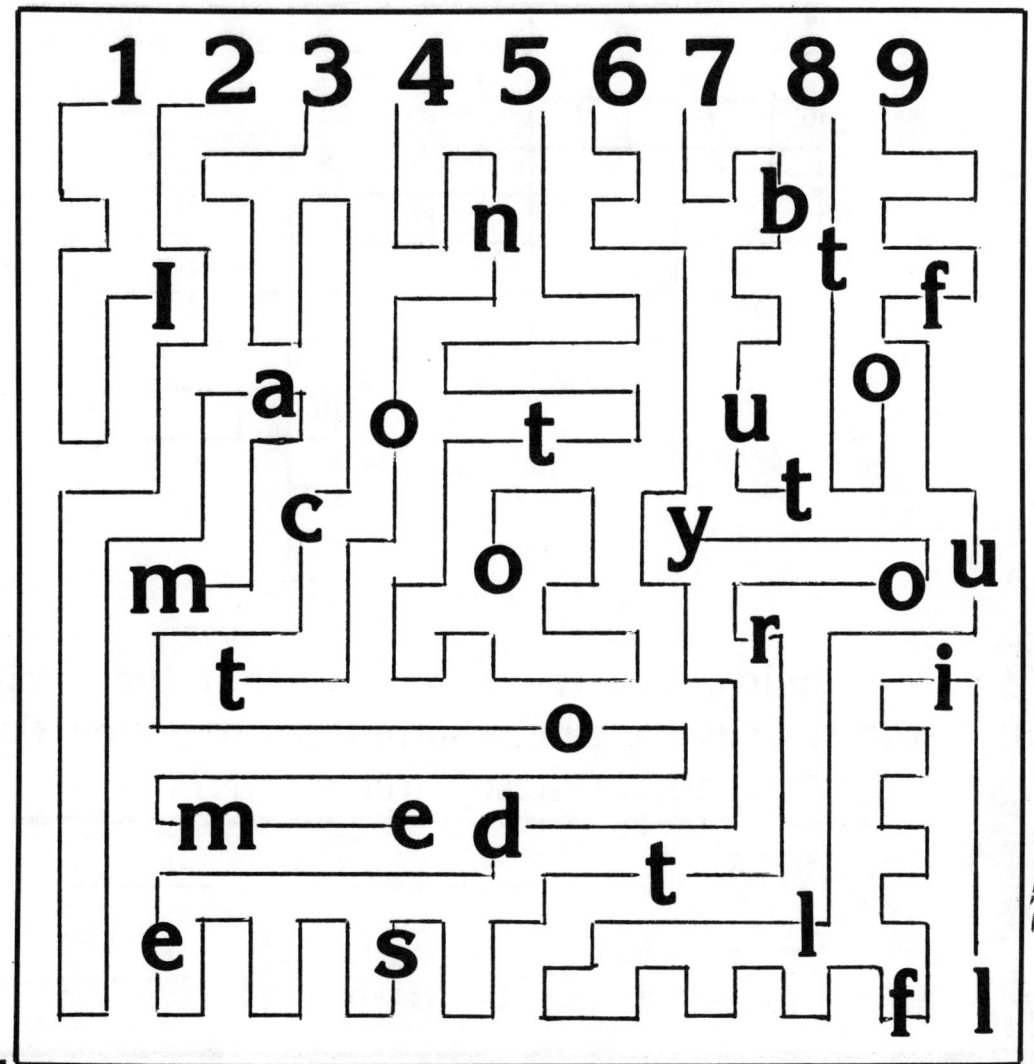

Name_____

Let the Scriptures help you solve this puzzle. Fill in the blanks with the correct words. Then place these words in the puzzle.

"Therefore if thou _ _ _ _ _ thy gift to the altar,

and there _ _ _ _ _ _ _ _ _ _ _ _ that thy

_ _ _ _ _ _ _ _ hath ought _ _ _ _ _ _ _ _

thee; _ _ _ _ _ there thy gift _ _ _ _ _ _ _ the

_ _ _ _ _ _ , and go _ _ _   _ _ _ ; first be

_ _ _ _ _ _ _ _ _ _ _ to thy brother, and then

_ _ _ _ and _ _ _ _ _ thy gift."

Matthew 5:23, 24

Below are three words from the Scriptures. They have been scrambled together. Can you unscramble these three words?

ANSWER: _ _ _ _ _ _ _   _ _ _ _ _ _

_ _ _ _ _

e e e a a a h d v n n r t h

Name _____

LOVE YOUR ENEMIES

Matthew 5:31-48

To discover the secret message, write the letter of the alphabet that comes before each letter found below.

Kftvt ubmlfe up uif qfpqmf boe

___ ___ ___ ___ ___

upme uifn ipx qfpqmf nvtu mjwf

___ ___ ___ ___ ___ ___

up cfmpoh up uif ljohepn pg Hpe.

___ ___ ___ ___ ___ ___ ___

If tbje tpnf jnqpsubou uijoht bcpvu

___ ___ ___ ___ ___ ___

uif xbz up usfbu uifjs fofnjft. If

___ ___ ___ ___ ___ ___ ___

tbje uifz tipvme mpwf uifjs fofnjft.

___ ___ ___ ___ ___ ___

LOVE YOUR ENEMIES!

Name_____

Finish these magic word squares by spelling words found in the Scriptures. The words must read down as well as across.

1.

k			
i			
s			
s			

2.

n	o	o	n

3.

d	u	l	l

4.

t			t
m			e

Make up your own magic word square using words found in the Scriptures.

Name_____

Shining Star Publication, Copyright © 1984, A division of Good Apple, Inc.

SERVICE AND PRAYER

Matthew 6:1-15

Each row of jumbled letters found below contains a hidden word. To discover the secret message, circle the hidden words and write them in the order they are found on the blanks below.

SECRET MESSAGE: "... ___ ___ ___ ___

___ ___ ___ ___ ___ ___ ___ ___

___ ___ ___ ___   ___ ___ ___ ___   ___—,

___ ___ ___ ___ ___ ___   ___ ___   ___ ___ ___

___ ___ ___ ."

```
G I M B H D C M Y O U R M F I D I
I T Y B F S V F A T H E R K E I M
K E T E W L N E E K N O W E T H E
W H A T M N B A E I M T Y R E A N
M B V E T H I N G S Y I U R R A M
M B Y E R V M O V X W Q R E N M R
B M C E W H A V E F E R T H M M N
I E B A F M N E E D I E E M T A O
E M T B T T M N V D V C O F W A E
B E F O R E W V M M T I M D N E I
H B V U M N V Y E S S S T A L O D
A S K M M X N B V C D E R T E R T
K M N N G I U Y I R T R M H I M S
```

Name_____

Find and circle every word from the Scripture hidden in the letter maze below. The words may be written down, across or diagonally.

". . . when thou prayest, enter into thy closet, and when thou has shut thy door, pray to thy Father which is in secret. . . ."

Matthew 6:6

```
W  T  W  H  E  N  I  S
P  H  F  A  T  H  E  R
R  O  E  W  H  I  C  R
A  U  A  N  D  I  N  B
Y  I  C  L  O  S  E  T
E  N  T  E  R  T  D  H
S  T  H  A  S  T  O  O
T  O  Y  S  H  H  O  U
P  R  A  Y  U  Y  R  D
S  E  C  R  T  H  Y  E
S  E  C  R  E  T  S  A
```

Begin in the lower right-hand box. Draw a continuous line from letter to letter, going left, right, up or down. You may not move diagonally. When you finish, the letters should form a sentence.

ANSWER: " . . . ___ ___   ___ ___ ___

___ ___ ___ ___ ___   ___

___ ___ ___ ___ ___ ___ ___ . . . . "

```
T  R  T  E  O  N
A  U  M  P  T  O
D  N  U  O  S  D
```

Name _____

Shining Star Publication, Copyright © 1984, A division of Good Apple, Inc.

JUDGE NOT

Matthew 7:1-23

To discover the secret message, follow the directions carefully.

"OKS,   OUE   IL   KHOTT   BD   GIVDU

_____ ___ __ _____ __ _____

YAN;   KDDS,   OUE   YD   KHOTT

___ _____ ___ __ _____

FIUE;   SUACS,   OUE   IL   KHOTT   BD

____ _____ ___ __ _____ __

APDUDE   NULA   YAN. . . ."

_____ ____ ___

Change all the A's to O's.
Change all the O's to A's.
Change all the S's to K's.
Change all the K's to S's.
Change all the U's to N's.
Change all the N's to U's.
Change all the E's to D's.
Change all the D's to E's.
Change all the L's to T's.
Change all the T's to L's.
The other letters are correct.

ASK, AND IT SHALL BE GIVEN YOU.

Name_____

To discover the secret message, write every other letter moving clockwise around the circle. You must decide where to begin.

SECRET MESSAGE: "_ _ _ _ _ _ _ _, _."

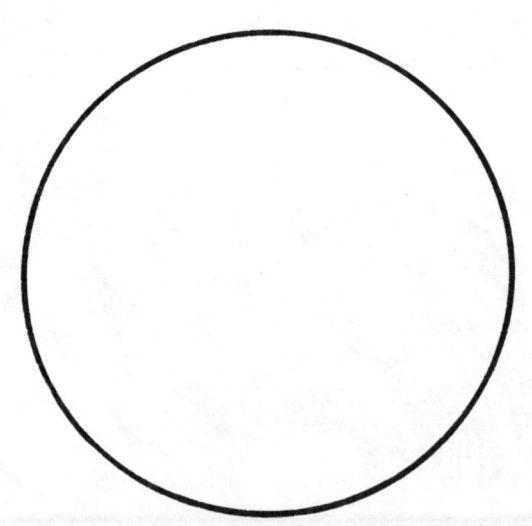

ETDYJEUBDEGNEONTOJTUTDHGA

HDGTOROEDEFBRRUINTGEEYTEHRRFYOGROTOH

SECRET MESSAGE: ". . . _ . . . ."

Make up your own circle puzzle using the Scriptures.

Name _____

Shining Star Publication, Copyright © 1984, A division of Good Apple, Inc.

COME UNTO ME

Matthew 11:1-9, 28-30

To discover the secret message, follow the directions carefully.

SECRET MESSAGE: " __ __ __ __   __ __ __ __
1 2 3 4   5 6 7 8

__ __ ' __ __ __   __ __   __ __ __ __
9 10   11 12 13   14 15   16 17 18 19

__ __ __ __ __ __   __ __ __   __ __ __
20 21 22 23 24 25   26 27 28   29 30 31

__ __ __ __ __   __ __ __ __ __ ' __ __ __
32 33 34 35 36   37 38 39 40 41   42 43 44

__   __ __ __ __   __ __ __ __   __ __ __
45   46 47 48 49   50 51 52 53   54 55 56

__ __ __ __ . "
57 58 59 60

Put the letter *a* in spaces 11, 18, 21, 26, 29, 34, 38 and 42.
Put the letter *b* in space 22.
Put the letter *c* in space 1.
Put the letter *d* in spaces 28, 39 and 44.
Put the letter *e* in spaces 4, 10, 15, 31, 33, 40, 53 and 58.
Put the letter *g* in space 50.
Put the letter *h* in spaces 17 and 32.
Put the letter *i* in spaces 45, 47 and 51.
Put the letter *l* in spaces 12, 13, 20, 37, 48 and 49.
Put the letter *m* in spaces 3 and 9.
Put the letter *n* in spaces 6, 27, 41 and 43.
Put the letter *o* in spaces 2, 8, 23 and 55.
Put the letter *r* in spaces 25, 30 and 57.
Put the letter *s* in space 59.
Put the letter *t* in spaces 7, 16, 19 and 60.
Put the letter *u* in spaces 5, 24 and 56.
Put the letter *v* in spaces 35 and 52.
Put the letter *w* in space 46.
Put the letter *y* in spaces 14, 36 and 54.

Name _____

The designs below are actually words.
Find the hidden letters in each design to form
words which will solve this puzzle.

ANSWER: "_ _ _ _ _

_ _ _ _ _ _ _ _ _ _ _ _ _ _

_ _ _ _ "

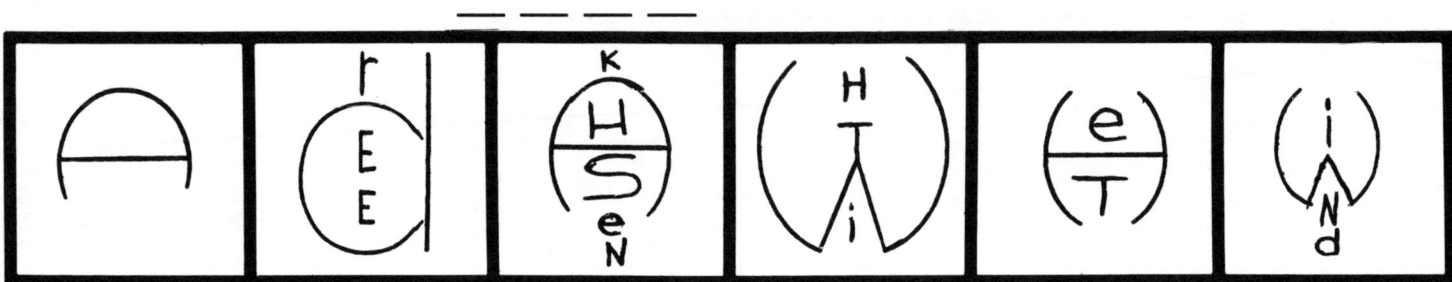

To discover the secret word you will need
your crayons. Color the spaces with one dot
PURPLE. Color the spaces with two dots
ORANGE.

Name_____

LORD OF THE SABBATH

Matthew 12:1-8; Mark 2:23-28; Luke 6:1-5

Find the shortest path through the maze. Color the path. To discover the message, write the letters in the order they are found.

SECRET MESSAGE: "∙ ∙ ∙ ___ ___ ___ ___   ___ ___ ___

___ ___ ___ ___ ___ ___ ___ ___ ___ ___

___ ___ ___ ___ ___   ___ ___   ___ ___ ___ ___

___ ___ ___ ___ ___ ___ ___   ___ ___ ___ ."

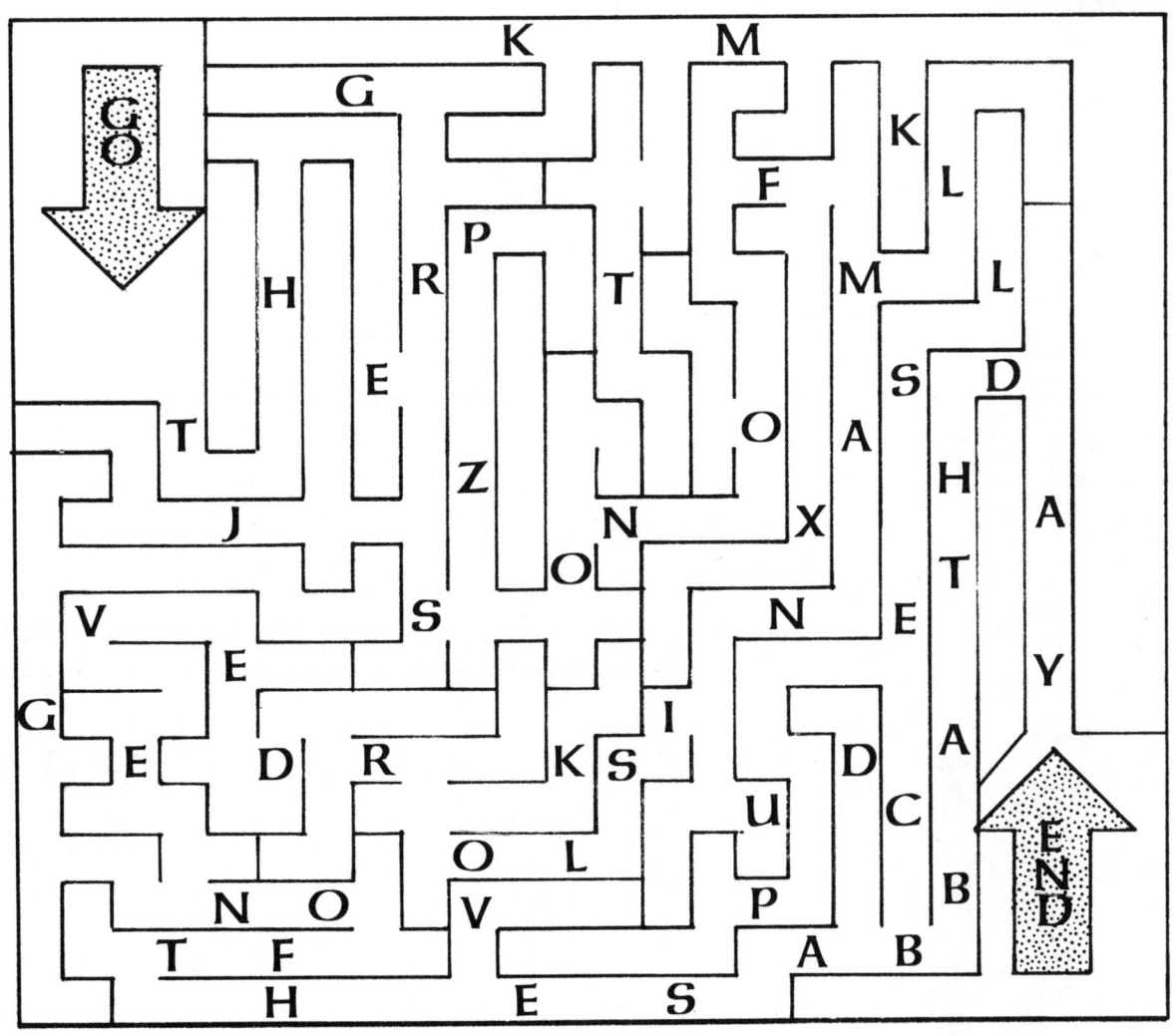

Shining Star Publication, Copyright © 1984, A division of Good Apple, Inc.

Complete these word stars by spelling
words found in the Scriptures. In each star the
words always have the same middle letter.

1.

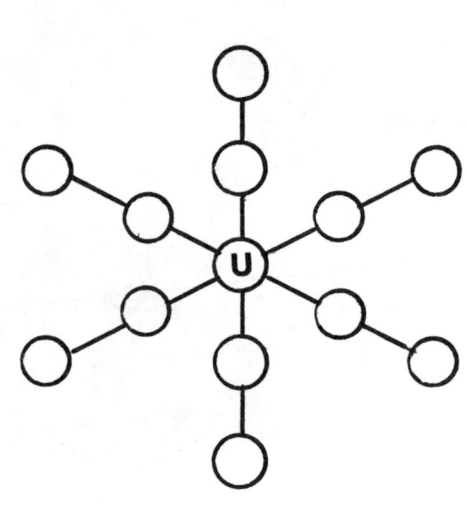

2.

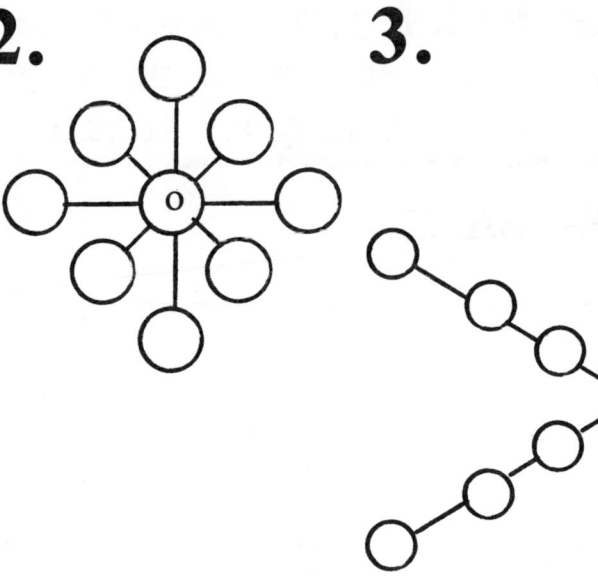

3.

Make up your own word star puzzle
using the Scriptures.

Three letters in this message have been
replaced with the letter *X*. Can you decode this
message by filling in the correct letters?

"XXVE   YE   NOT   REXX   WXXT

_____   __   ___   ____   ____

XXVIX   XIX. . . ."

_____   __

Name_____

GREATEST IN THE KINGDOM

Matthew 18:1-10; Mark 9:33-37; Luke 9:46-48

Cross out one letter in each word below to spell a new word and discover the answer to this puzzle. Then write your own message and put one extra letter in each word. Ask a friend to solve your puzzle.

SWHEN   LASKED,   "WHOM   HIS   THEN

_____ _____ _____ _____ _____

GREATESTE   INN   THEM   KINGDOME   OFF

_____ _____ _____ _____ _____

SHEAVEN?"   JESSUS   CAELLED   AS   SLITTLE

_____ _____ _____ _____ _____

CHIELD   TUNTO   SHIM.   THE   SEAT   THEN

_____ _____ _____ _____ _____ _____

CHILDS   TIN   THEM   MOIDDLE   OFF   STHEM

_____ _____ _____ _____ _____ _____

SAND   SLAID,   "WHOSOEVERS   THEREFOURE

_____ _____ _____ _____

SHALLT   HUMMBLE   HIMSLELF   HAS   THIES

_____ _____ _____ _____ _____

SLITTLE   CHEILD,   THEN   SAIME   HIS

_____ _____ _____ _____ _____

GREATTEST   INN   THEN   SKINGDOM   OFF

_____ _____ _____ _____ _____

HEAVENS."

_____

All the vowels in the message below are incorrect. Replace the incorrect vowels with the correct vowels, and you will discover the secret message.

"...VARELY A SEY INTA YAI, AXCUPT YA

___ _ ___ ___ ___ ___

BO CANVIRTUD, END BOCAMI ES LETTLA

__ _____ ___ _____ __ _____

CHULDRAN, YA SHOLL NET INTUR UNTA

_____ __ ____ ___ _____ ____

THU KENGDUM IF HOEVON."

___ _____ __ _____

Circle the first letter and then circle every third letter to discover the answer to this puzzle.

ANSWER: "_ _ _ _ _ _ _
_ _ _ _ _ _ _ _ _ _ _ _ _ _ _
_ _ _ _ _ _ _ _ _ _ _ _ _ _
_ _ _ _ _ _ _ _ _ _ _ _ _ _ _,
_ _ _ _ _ _ _ _ _ _ _ _ _ _ _ _
_ _ _ _ _ _ _ _ _ _ _ _
_ _ _ _ _ _."

W t y h e i o p i s k j o m n e v n v u i e n b r g h
t b v h m c e h g r t y e m b f t r o u y r m c e e w
s g h h x c a r e l y t l o p h t r u n b m s d b w q
l r t e v c h y t i b v m s e s r t e m n l r e f b v
a u t s i t t b v h r e i m n s c v l t y i t r t m n
t g h l e r e c n c g h h w c i r e l b v d r t t h e
h e r e x x s w e a m n m e r e t y i w e s d e g x r
r g h e r t a u y t r e e u y s m n t m n i e w n i u
t m n h r t e i n k i u i b n n r t g w q d i o o e b
m i r o t y f h i h a s e g h a u i v r e e t y n h g

Name_____

TWO OR THREE ARE GATHERED

Matthew 18:15-20

To decode this message, use the code found below. The letter *V* is found once in the message.

I	E	F
B	T	H
S	G	A

Y	L	R
D	Q	M
U	N	P

Name_____

Begin in the upper left-hand corner and end in the lower right-hand corner. Find a path through the letters that spells a message. You must move across or down. You may not move diagonally.

___

SECRET MESSAGE: ＿＿＿＿＿ ＿＿

＿ ＿＿ ＿＿＿ ＿＿＿＿＿ ＿＿

＿＿＿＿."

```
T H E R E T H T T T T T
H E R A H H E H H H H H
E R E M T H E R E A M I I
R E I I I N I N T H E M I
E A M I I N N T H E M I S
A M H I T T E R E I N T S
M I E N H H M I S T S H A
I T R T E E M I D S O E T
I I E H M I D S S T O F T
N N I E M I S T A M I T H
T T N T H E M I S T A M E
H E M I S T H E R E I N M
```

Can you find 12 words in the Scriptures that have homonyms? Write each word and list its homonym.

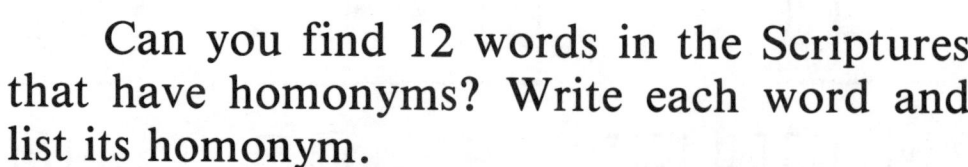

1.＿＿＿＿＿＿＿＿	7.＿＿＿＿＿＿＿＿
2.＿＿＿＿＿＿＿＿	8.＿＿＿＿＿＿＿＿
3.＿＿＿＿＿＿＿＿	9.＿＿＿＿＿＿＿＿
4.＿＿＿＿＿＿＿＿	10.＿＿＿＿＿＿＿＿
5.＿＿＿＿＿＿＿＿	11.＿＿＿＿＿＿＿＿
6.＿＿＿＿＿＿＿＿	12.＿＿＿＿＿＿＿＿

Name＿＿＿＿＿＿＿＿＿＿＿＿＿＿＿＿＿＿＿

THE LITTLE CHILDREN

Matthew 19:13-15; Mark 10:13-16; Luke 18:15-17

Decode the secret message. Some of the letters have been replaced with numbers. You must decide which letters stand for which numbers.

C = __   D = __   N = __   R = __   S = __   T = __

O7e   2ay   5ome   mo6he45   b4ough6   6hei4

___   ___   ____   _____   _____   _____

3hil24e7   6o   5ee   Je5u5.   6he   2i53iple5   56a46e2   6o

_____   __   ___   _____   ___   _____   _____   __

5e72   6he   3hil24e7   away.   Je5u5   5ai2,   "Le6   6he

____   ___   _____   _____   _____   ____   ___   ___

3hil24e7   3ome   6o   me."

_____   ____   __   ___

Shining Star Publication, Copyright © 1984, A division of Good Apple, Inc.

To discover the secret message, follow the directions carefully.

SECRET MESSAGE: "_ _ _ _ _ _

_ _ _ _ _ _   _ _ _ _ _ _ _ _,   _ _ _

_ _ _ _ _ _   _ _ _ _   _ _ _,   _ _

_ _ _   _ _ _ _   _ _: _ _ _   _ _ _

_ _ _ _ _   _ _ _ _   _ _ _   _ _ _ _ _ _

_ _   _ _ _ _ _ _."

1. S U F F E R J A N E L I T T L E
2. O X C H I L D R E N A N D R E W
3. C H R I S T Y A N D Y E L L O W
4. A M A R K F O R B I D S E V E N
5. B Z T H E M E L I Z A B E T H Z
6. N O T R E D T O J O H N F O U R
7. C O L T C O M E N A O M I Z Z S
8. U N T O K A T H Y Z Z Z M E E
9. F O R T E N O F C A T S U C H V
10. W I L L I A M I S F I S H T H E
11. K I N G D O M S A R A H Z Z O F
12. S I L V E R H E A V E N F I V E

Cross out the girl's name in lines 1, 3, 5, 7, 8 and 11.
Cross out the boy's name in lines 2, 4, 6 and 10.
Cross out the color in lines 3, 6 and 12.
Cross out the number in lines 4, 6, 9 and 12.
Cross out the animal in lines 2, 7, 9 and 10.
Cross out the first letter in lines 4 and 5.
Cross out the last letter in lines 7, 8 and 9.
Cross out all the "Z's" in the puzzle.

Below are three words from the Scriptures. They have been scrambled together. Can you unscramble these three words?

ANSWER: "... _ _ _ _ _ _ _

_ _ _ _   _ _ _...."

T I H N O O F R B D E M T

Name_____

RICH YOUNG RULER

Matthew 19:16-26

Complete each word by adding one letter.
The words are all found in the Scriptures. Then
read down to discover the secret message.

SECRET MESSAGE: "... _ _ _ _
_ _ _   _ _ _   _ _ _ _ _ _
_ _ _   _ _ _ _ _ _ _ _."

__hy	th__t	m__n
__s	fo__low	ente__
__here	__ove	cam__l
__e		
	__reasure	disci__les
__o	__eaven	wh__
th__u	__n	__aved
sai__	you__g	__aying
	__reat	eas__er
	Je__us	__eheld
		al__
		amaz__d

Name_____

Shining Star Publication, Copyright © 1984, A division of Good Apple, Inc.

"...It is EZR 4 a 2 through the of a , than 4 a rich 2 N + TR into the + dom of GOD."

Matthew 19:24

Name _____

JUDGMENT

Matthew 25:31-46

To discover the secret message, use the consonants listed below and complete the words. Cross out each letter when you have used it.

L N R S T V Y Y Y

"... _e_i__ I _a_ u__o _ou,

C D F F H H H H L M N N N N S S S S T T T T T V Y

I__a__u__ a_ _e _a_e _o_e

i__ u__o o_e o_ __e _ea__

o_ __e_e

B D H H M M N N N R R T T T V Y Y

__ __e___e_, _e _a_e _o_e

 i_ u__o _e."

Name_____

The letter designs below are actually scrambled words. Each design is a different word. Unscramble the words to discover the secret message.

SECRET MESSAGE: "... _ _ _ _

_ _ _ _ _ _ _ _ _ _ _

_ _ _ _ _ _ _ _ _ _ _

_ _ _ _ _ _ _ _ _ _."

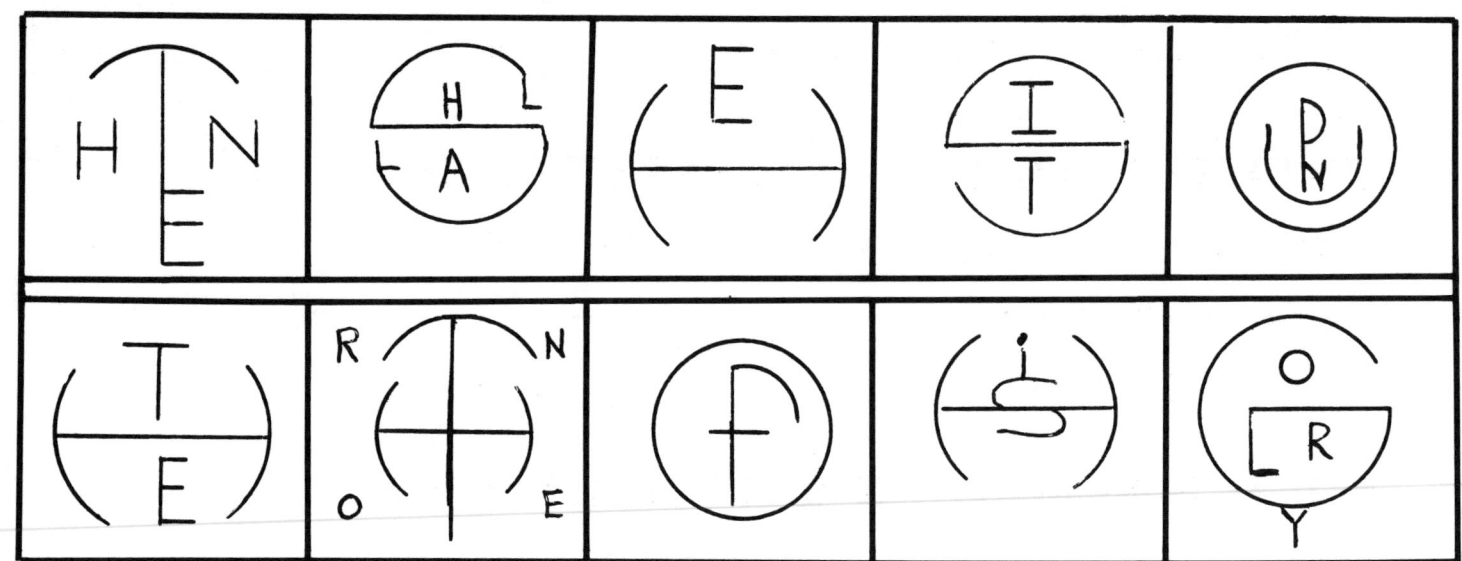

What word found in the Scriptures can you put in the middle that makes three-letter words of the letters going down?

a	p	a	t	a	s	t	o	a
m	g	e	e	e	t	e	t	k

Name_____

Shining Star Publication, Copyright © 1984, A division of Good Apple, Inc.

REVIEW

Matthew 25:31-46

Begin in any circle. Move along circles that are connected by a line. How many words found in Matthew 25:31-46 can you spell? There are at least 30.

_____ _____ _____ _____ _____
_____ _____ _____ _____ _____
_____ _____ _____ _____ _____
_____ _____ _____ _____ _____
_____ _____ _____ _____ _____

```
T   N   D   L   U   P   E   U
T   N   D   L   U   P   E   U
H   E   A   L   O   N   E   N
W   S   H   G   R   H   T   A
O   N   I   M   Y   S   G   O
F   I   H   O   L   I   N   K
A   N   G   E   T   F   I   D
W   T   C   O   M   R   D   Y
I   H   A   N   A   O   O   U
```

Name_____

PRE AND POST-TEST

Read the statements below. If the statement is true, color the appropriately numbered spaces PINK. If the statement is false, color the appropriately numbered spaces BLACK.

1. Jesus went into the wilderness for thirty days and thirty nights.
2. The devil came to tempt Jesus while He was in the wilderness.
3. The devil offered the world to Jesus if Jesus would just bow down to him.
4. Jesus told the devil, "Get thee hence, Satan."
5. Jesus said, "Blessed are the peacemakers: for they shall inherit the earth."
6. Jesus said, "Blessed are the pure in heart: for they shall see God."
7. Jesus said, "Your Father knoweth what things ye have need of before ye ask him."
8. Jesus said, "An eye for an eye and a tooth for a tooth."
9. Jesus said that children are the greatest in the kingdom of heaven.
10. Jesus said, "If your brother trespasses against you, go and tell him his fault."
11. Jesus said, "It is easier for a camel to go through the eye of a needle than for a rich man to enter the kingdom of God."
12. Jesus said, "With God all things are possible."

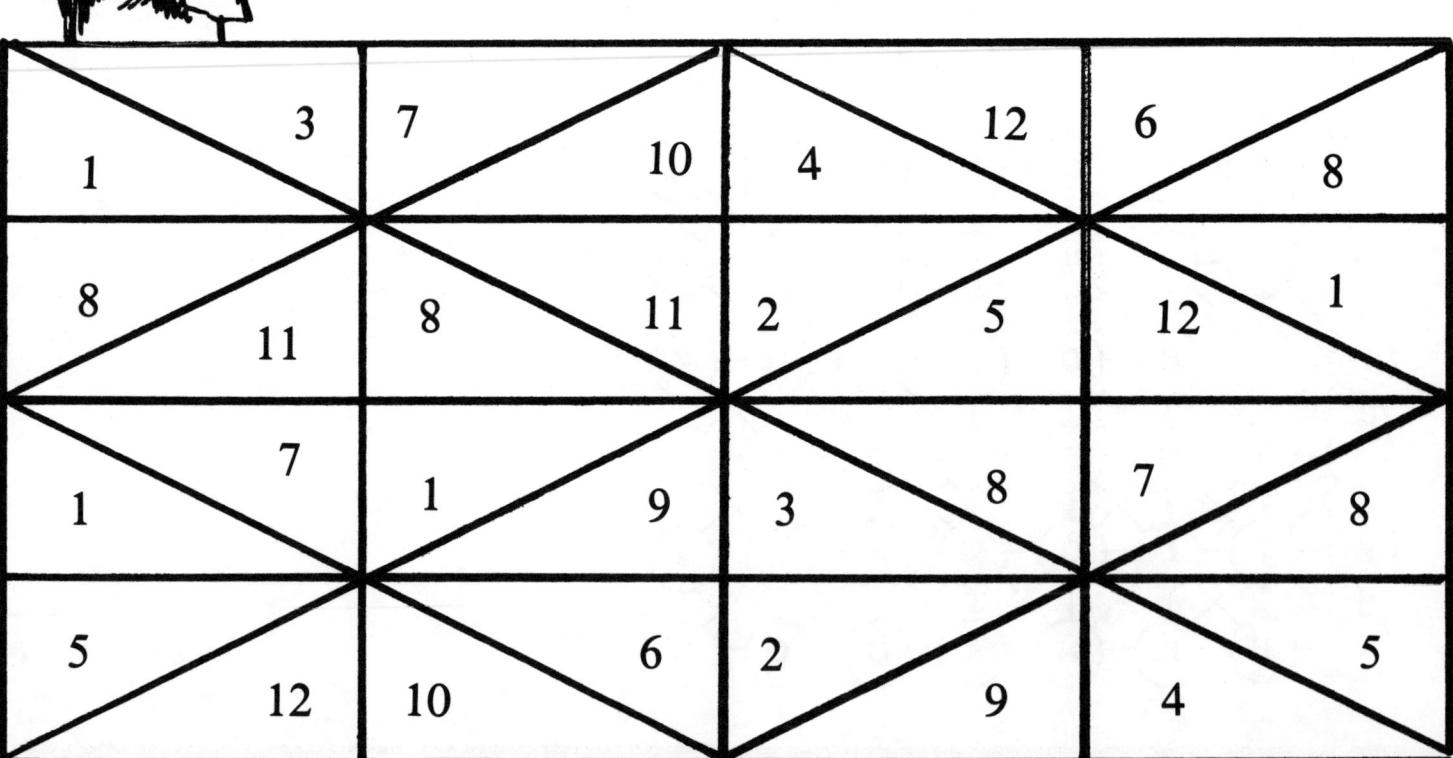

Name_____

3. "Man shall not live by bread alone."
"Thou shalt not tempt the Lord thy God."
"Get thee hence, Satan."

4. Across:
 1. worship
 3. devil
 5. unto
 6. angels
 9. ministered

Down:
 1. written
 2. serve
 4. leaveth
 7. shalt
 8. him

temptation

5. "And seeing the multitudes, he went up into a mountain: and when he was set, his disciples came unto him: And he opened his mouth, and taught them. . . ."

6. GOD
poor in spirit-kingdom of heaven; they that mourn-comforted; meek-the earth; hunger and thirst for righteousness-shall be filled; merciful-obtain mercy; pure in heart-shall see God; peacemakers-called the children of God

the, when, are, earth, that, was, see, were, set, he, went, and, heart

7. I am come not to destroy, but to fulfil.

8. "Therefore if thou bring thy gift to the altar, and there rememberest that thy brother hath ought against thee; Leave there thy gift before the altar, and go thy way; first be reconciled to thy brother, and then come and offer thy gift."

Across:
 1. rememberest
 5. way
 6. against
 9. before
 10. bring
 11. offer
 12. come

Down:
 2. brother
 3. thy
 4. leave
 7. altar
 8. reconciled

heaven and earth

9. Jesus talked to the people and told them how people must live to belong to the kingdom of God. He said some important things about the way to treat their enemies. He said they should love their enemies.

10.
```
k i n g     r i s e
i     o     a     v
s     o     i     e
s a i d     n o o n
g i v e     t h a t
o     v     h     h
o     i     e     e
d u l l     m i l e
```

11. ". . . YOUR FATHER KNOWETH WHAT THINGS YE HAVE NEED OF, BEFORE YE ASK HIM."

12.
```
W T   W H E N   I S
P H   F A T H E R R
R O   E W H I C H B
A U   A N D I N B T
Y I   C L O S E T H
E N   T E R T D O O
S T   H A S T H O U
T O   Y S H T Y R D
P R A Y   H U Y   D
S E C R E T H Y   E
S E C R E T S   A
```

". . . Do not sound a trumpet . . . ."

13. "Ask, and it shall be given you; seek, and ye shall find; knock, and it shall be opened unto you . . . ."

14. "Judge not, that ye be not judged."
". . . every good tree bringeth forth good fruit . . . ."

15. "Come unto me, all ye that labour and are heavy laden, and I will give you rest."

16. "A reed shaken with the wind"
JOHN

17. ". . . THE SON OF MAN IS LORD EVEN OF THE SABBATH DAY."

18. 1. pluck, house, would
 2. not, how, God, for or Son
 3. priests, entered, blameless

"Have ye not read what David did . . . ."

19. When asked, "Who is the greatest in the kingdom of heaven?" Jesus called a little child unto Him. He set the child in the middle of them and said, "Whosoever therefore shall humble himself as this little child, the same is greatest in the kingdom of heaven."

20. ". . . Verily I say unto you, Except ye be converted, and become as little children, ye shall not enter into the kingdom of heaven."
"Whosoever therefore shall humble himself as this little child, the same is greatest in the kingdom of heaven."

21. "If your brother trespasses against you, go and tell him his fault. If he listens to you, then you have gained a brother."

22. ". . . there am I in the midst of them."

```
T H E R E T H T T T T T
H E R A H H E H H H H H
R E E M T H E R E A M I I
E A M I I N T H E M I S
A M H I T T E R E I N T S
M I E N H H M I S T S H A
I T R T E E M I D S O F T
I I E H M I D S T O F T
N N I E M I S T A M I T H
T T N T H E M I S T A M E
H E M I S T H E R E I N M
```

him, hymn; hear, here; not, knot; one, won; two, to, too; in, inn; be, bee; I, eye; you, ewe, yew; for, four; thee, the; done, dun

23. c = 3, d = 2, n = 7, r = 4, s = 5, t = 6
One day some mothers brought their children to see Jesus. The disciples started to send the children away. Jesus said, "Let the children come to me."

24. "Suffer little children, and forbid them not, to come unto me: for of such is the kingdom of heaven."
". . . forbid them not . . . ."

25. ". . . with God all things are possible."

26. ". . . It is easier for a camel to go through the eye of a needle than for a rich man to enter into the kingdom of God."

27. ". . . Verily I say unto you, Inasmuch as ye have done it unto one of the least of these my brethren, ye have done it unto me."

28. ". . . then shall he sit upon the throne of his glory."
righteous

29. when, Son, of, man, shall, come, it, his, glory, and, all, the, holy, angels, with, him, then, he, sit, upon, throne, one, from, sheep, goats, king, drink, you, did, in, unto

30. true: 2, 3, 4, 6, 7, 9, 10, 11, 12
 false: 1, 5, 8

AWARD CERTIFICATE

This is to certify that

_____

has successfully completed a study of Jesus, the
teacher. The Scriptures covered
Matthew 3:13-17, 4:1-17, 5:1-48, 6:1-15, 7:1-23,
11:1-30, 12:1-8, 18:1-20, 19:13-26, 25:31-46;
Mark 1:9-11, 2:23-28, 4:21-23, 9:33-37, 10:13-16;
Luke 3:21,22, 6:1-49, 9:46-48, 18:15-17.

_____
signature (teacher)

_____
signature (pastor)

_____
date